Foundations of Biblical Inerrancy

David R. Nicholas

BMH Books
Winona Lake, Indiana 46590

ISBN: 0-88469-104-7

COPYRIGHT 1978
BMH BOOKS
WINONA LAKE, INDIANA

PRINTED IN U.S.A.

Foreword

The inerrancy of Scripture is absolutely essential to Christianity. This is true for at least two reasons. First, Christ and the apostles taught this doctrine (cf. Matt. 5:18; II Tim. 3:16, etc.). Therefore, if the Bible is not what they said it is, then they either lied or were mistaken—and in either case the entire foundation of Christianity collapses (cf. Eph. 2:20). In the second place, a Bible that is not completely inerrant is hopelessly untrustworthy, because no one could be sure that what he reads in the Bible is an errant portion. One would have to be omniscient to know which words are correct and which are not correct. Only if *all* Scripture is true can it be confidently read and obeyed.

Mr. David Nicholas has done a commendable piece of work by bringing this problem into focus in this study. It is my prayer that God may use it for His glory and for the encouragement of His people everywhere.

> John C. Whitcomb
> Professor of Theology
> Grace Theological Seminary
>
> June 1, 1978

DEDICATION

This book is affectionately dedicated to my loving wife, Donna, whose ministry to me and to our two daughters, Joy and Faith, makes my ministry possible.

Table of Contents

INTRODUCTION 7
    The Problem
    The Purpose
    The Procedure
    The Precaution

Chapter 1—THE FOUNDATION OF SEMANTIC CONSISTENCY ... 9
    Objections to Inerrancy
    The Proper Understanding of Inerrancy

Chapter 2—THE FOUNDATION OF HISTORICAL TESTIMONY ... 15
    The Consensus of the Church Fathers
        Origen
        Irenaeus
        Justin Martyr
        Polycarp and Clement
        Josephus
        Chrysostom
        Augustine
    The Consensus of the Reformers
        Luther
        Calvin

Chapter 3—THE FOUNDATION OF SCRIPTURAL TESTIMONY .. 35
    John 10:34-36
    II Timothy 3:16
    II Peter 1:20-21

CONCLUSION 44

ENDNOTES 45

BIBLIOGRAPHY 49

Introduction

The Problem

The publication of Harold Lindsell's *The Battle for the Bible* has surfaced an evangelical conflict over the extent of Biblical reliability that has been simmering for some time.

Latent particularly within the Neo-Evangelical movement over the past 20 years there has been increasing resistance to the concept of Biblical inerrancy; and inerrancy, as it is conceived by many conservative evangelicals and fundamentalists, has been called into question and labeled as out of step with classical Christian tradition. Biblical inerrancy, as commonly understood today, is linked rather with post-Reformation scholastic orthodoxy typified by B. B. Warfield and Charles Hodge. This particular brand of orthodoxy is said to have widely influenced the ecclesiastical associations and organizations which were born in the wake of the Fundamentalist/Modernist controversy.[1] The opponents of inerrancy contend that Biblical authority is best understood in terms of "faith and practice," and should not be equated with "error-free statements" in relation to history, science, geography and chronology. The word "inerrancy" is viewed as anachronistic, and is viewed by many of the "errancy" advocates as "not a very helpful word since it is a modern standard of precision and scientific accuracy."[2] As understood today, it is not seen as descriptive of classical Christian thought on Biblical accuracy.

According to the inerrancy advocates, however, such arguments are merely attempts to appease the intellectual and rationalistic mind-set of those who are obsessed with the idea that there must be a minimum of inexplicable conflict between science, history, geography and Scripture, for fear that an undue emphasis on inerrancy will "encourage people to avoid the real issues and serve to drive young, clearheaded students away from evangelicalism into the liberal camp."[3] John Warwick Montgomery represents well the position of inerrancy advocates when he writes:

> Whenever we reach the point of affirming on the one hand that the Bible is infallible or inerrant and admitting on the other hand to internal contradictions or factual inaccuracies within it,

we not only make a farce of language, promoting ambiguity, confusion, and perhaps even deception in the church; more reprehensible than even these things, we in fact deny the plenary inspiration and authority of Scripture, regardless of the theological formulae we may insist on retaining.[4]

The Purpose

It is the objective of this study to determine whether inerrancy, as alleged by some, is merely a post-Reformation phenomenon, or whether it is indeed a legitimate theological concept which is rooted in Scripture and reflected in the writings of church history from the Church Fathers to the Reformers.

The Procedure

In accordance with the purpose of this study, the writer intends to consider in order what he holds to be three important foundations of Biblical inerrancy: The foundation of semantic consistency, a discussion of the proper understanding of the term "inerrancy" as it relates to Scripture; the foundation of historical testimony, an examination of the flow of thought concerning the nature and authority of Scripture down through the history of the church; and the foundation of scriptural testimony, a historical-grammatical analysis of key passages which teach the Scripture's view of itself.

The Precaution

While an attempt is made to evaluate the positions of prominent Church Fathers and leading Reformers on the basis of primary sources when accessible, it is imperative that the reader understand the statements of the various individuals quoted to be statements of fallible men. They are not inspired statements and consequently cannot be considered tantamount to Scripture. Whether they appear supportive or nonsupportive of inerrancy, in the final analysis it is the testimony of Scripture itself which must ultimately determine its nature. Any attempt to discount, redefine or explain away the Bible's testimony to its own nature in an attempt to make Scripture more credible is in reality to impugn the credibility of God's Word—clearly a self-defeating effort.

Chapter 1

The Foundation of Semantic Consistency

The conflict over the mode and result of Biblical inspiration centers basically around the meaning of the term "inerrancy." Generally the terms "inerrant," "infallible," "true," and "trustworthy" have been taken as synonymous, and when used with reference to Scripture they have been indicative of the absolute reliability of a product which originated with God. To use the term "inerrant" has been to ascertain that Scripture is "without error" as God revealed it to man. To employ the term "infallible" has been to declare that the Scripture is incapable of being erroneous or false. To describe the Bible as "trustworthy" has been to affirm one's reliance on its integrity and reliability. To speak of the Bible as "true" has been to equate Scripture with this attribute of the God by whom it is inspired in accordance with scriptural teaching that He is a "true witness" (Rev. 3:14), and that His Word is "true from the beginning" (Ps. 119:160). During the past 25 years, however, a growing evangelical uneasiness has developed over the use of the word "inerrant" in relation to Scripture.

Objections to Inerrancy

David Allan Hubbard, president of Fuller Theological Seminary, has recently protested that inerrancy "implies a precision alien to the minds of the Bible writers and their own use of the Scriptures."[5] He holds that inerrancy is too precise and too mathematical a term to describe adequately the way in which God's infallible revelation has come to us in a book. Such protests can only imply that there are inconsistencies, problems and even contradictions in the scriptural text that amount to errors, an implication which in the context of contemporary thought does a great deal to undermine general confidence in the Bible.

To further complicate the problem, William Sanford La Sor, professor of Old Testament at Fuller Seminary, equates scriptural statements taken apart from their context with Biblical errors simply because, although accurately recorded, they represent falsehoods uttered by Satan or Job's friends. In speaking of his objection to the phrase, "and are without error in the whole and in the part," in the original Fuller Theological Seminary Statement of Faith, La Sor writes:

> I objected to that statement insisting that the Scriptures are *not* without error *in the part*. In fact, there are many statements in the Bible which, taken apart from their context, are clearly erroneous. In addition to such obvious examples as the lies of Satan, the false statements of Job's friends, and other erroneous declarations, there are such matters as altered prophecy (such as that of Micaiah ben Imlah), and judgments of God that are later altered by God's "changing His mind."[6]

The above statement of La Sor must represent a "new low" in the proper understanding of "inerrancy" as it relates to Scripture, for the classical Christian understanding of "without error in the part" is that every "part" of God's inspired Word is true and not subject to doubt, as will be certified later in this study.

It is difficult to understand how such obvious admissions of scriptural error can be squared with belief in Biblical infallibility; nevertheless, in speaking for the faculty of Fuller Seminary, Hubbard writes: "we stand in full fellowship with the Apostles, the reformers, and the evangelical missioners of the centuries. None of us denies the infallibility of the Bible . . . ."[7] Hubbard's statement of the Fuller faculty's belief in "infallibility" is obviously conditional to the judgment of which *parts* of the scriptural text are infallible.

In order to justify the linguistic gymnastics required to accept the Bible's infallibility while denying its inerrancy, Hubbard and others appeal to the Reformation teaching that "the internal testimony of the Holy Spirit is the proof of Scripture's authority." He states:

> ... we do not have to establish the trustworthiness of the Scripture before we can proclaim the Gospel. In a sense, the truth of the Gospel takes historical priority to the Scriptures. The Word of God to the Apostles and Prophets was truth in and of itself long before the scriptures were completed as the Reformed creeds often acknowledged. What proof did the prophets need to test whether God was speaking to them? Nothing but the power of the Word itself . . . .[8]

Thus, because the Word of God is "powerful" and "self-authenticating," inerrancy is denied as excess theological baggage, irrelevant to the issue of scriptural authority.

Aside from the Barthian flavor of such reasoning and its incomplete representation of Reformation thought on the matter of scriptural authority, it is at best offensive to clear thinking. While it is certainly true that there is no necessity to establish the trustworthiness of the Scripture before proclaiming the Gospel; and while it is correct to say that the truth of the Gospel takes *historical* priority over the Scriptures, it does not logically follow that evangelical theologians are thereby justified in playing fast and loose with the accuracy of God's "inscripturated" Word! It is the written Word which for us today is inspired, and it is on the basis of this written Word alone that the facts of the Gospel are verified in detail. Sproul, commenting on the impossibility of Biblical error, writes:

> What is at issue is not the question whether or not human beings can err. What is at issue is the question whether or not God inspires error or the Holy Spirit guides into error. When orthodoxy confesses the infallibility of Scripture, it is not confessing anything about the intrinsic infallibility of men. Rather, the confession rests its confidence on the integrity of God. On numerous occasions I have queried several Biblical and theological scholars in the following manner—"Do you maintain the inerrancy of Scripture?"—"No"—"Do you believe the Bible to be inspired of God?"—"Yes"—"Do you think God in-

Foundations of Biblical Inerrancy / 11

spires error?"—"No"—"Is all the Bible inspired by God?"—"Yes"—"Is the Bible errant?"—"No"—"Is it inerrant?"—"No"—At that point I usually acquire an excedrin headache.[9]

Hubbard asks, "Can we let the Bible be what it is?"[10] We answer with an enthusiastic "yes!" Let us allow it to be the product of a God of integrity and truth, and let's not quibble over whether we call it "inerrant" or "infallible," for it is incongruous, no matter how one cuts it, to equate error with the product of a God of integrity and truth. Furthermore, if we take the Reformers' viewpoint, does it really matter if science, geography or history seems to contradict Biblical data? A presuppositional approach to Scripture accepts the final authority of God's Word no matter what! Is our confidence in the Bible so shallow that we cannot allow it to speak for itself in matters related to science, history and geography? Is it really necessary to embark on exercises of linguistic gymnastics so as to conserve our intellectual and academic image in the eyes of the secular, unbelieving world? Granted, the Bible is not a textbook of science, history or geography. But by the same token, can we expect a God of integrity and truth to inspire statements which, when properly understood and interpreted, are less than accurate in these areas? Logic alone would dictate a negative answer to these questions. However, we are not left with logic alone, for in recent years archaeology has confirmed with regularity the accuracy of historical, geographical and chronological aspects of God's Word. In addition, research in the field of scientific creationism has shaken the very foundation of evolutionary thought and theory, making it far more logical to accept a creationist view on origins in keeping with the Biblical record. Is it not far better to begin with the presupposition of scriptural inerrancy as did Augustine, and leave it to God to reveal in His own time explanations to those scriptural problems which we cannot explain? Augustine leaves no doubt as to his belief in inerrancy, for in a letter to his friend, Jerome, he writes:

> For I confess to your charity that I have learned to yield this respect and honor only to the canonical books of Scripture: of

these alone do I most firmly believe that the authors were completely free from error. And if in these writings I am perplexed by anything which appears to me opposed to the truth, I do not hesitate to suppose that either the manuscript is faulty, or the translator has not caught the meaning of what was said, or I myself have failed to understand it.[11]

The Proper Understanding of Inerrancy

What should fundamentalists and conservative evangelicals mean by the term, "inerrancy"? Unfortunately, many well-meaning, Bible-believing Christians cannot provide an adequate answer to this question. However, this fact in no way justifies the charge of various anti-inerrancy advocates that to believe in inerrancy narrows one's concept of inspiration to that of mechanical dictation. Warfield, the acknowledged authority on inerrancy, certainly did not take this view for he carefully writes, "it ought to be unnecessary to protest again against the habit of representing the advocates of 'verbal inspiration' as teaching that the mode of inspiration was by dictation."[12]

Granted, in the heat of battle against the higher critics there were rationalistic attempts to uphold the accuracy of Scripture which led some well-meaning individuals to needlessly overreact to such charges, not finding themselves content to rest on their presuppositions while the enemy rationalistically demolished their beloved book before the eyes of the world. The Reformers never really faced such a calculated assault on the integrity of Scripture, and consequently, they were never forced to credalize their position on the details of scriptural authority as it related to inerrancy. However, it is difficult to imagine that even the apostles themselves would have allowed such a challenge to go unrefuted. Undoubtedly, the Apostle Peter was concerned with the integrity of Scripture when he clarified the origin of both his own teaching as well as that of Scripture in I Peter 1:16–21.

The fact that there have been misunderstandings as to the proper understanding of Biblical inerrancy should not, however, disqualify this historic term from being included in our theological vocabulary, for inerrancy postulates only that "each writer who was borne of the Holy Spirit has recorded accurately that which the Spirit desired him to record. The Bible, in other words, is a true account of those things of which it speaks."[13] A responsible view of the doctrine of inerrancy does not demand the literal interpretation of Scripture where literary devices demand otherwise. It does not require that the Biblical writers be viewed as mere "automata"; it does not insist that Biblical writers in recording the same event must be in actual verbal agreement with one another. It does not demand that narrated events be in the same order, for there are times when, for the sake of emphasis, the order is not intended to be chronological. Inerrancy does not insist that when two writers translate from another language, their translations should agree verbatim. It allows them freedom of expression, as long as they represent accurately the thought of the original. Inerrancy does not imply that each writer must give the details or even as many details of the same event as another writer, nor does it require that each writer must view the same event from precisely the same standpoint. Inerrancy allows for the full employment of the gifts and talents with which God endowed the human writer.[14]

In summary, God so superintended the writing of Scripture that what He intended to be written was written the way He wanted it to be written, through prepared human instruments with all their inadequacies and failings. This is the sense in which the Bible must be considered inerrant or infallible. There is no logical inconsistency in ascribing "inerrancy" to a written product so communicated to men.

But what of the charges that "inerrancy" is not the historic Christian view of Scripture, but rather a post-Reformation phenomenon? This question we shall take up in the following chapter.

Chapter 2

The Foundation of Historical Testimony

The Consensus of the Church Fathers

As one examines the writings of the Church Fathers, particularly the ante-Nicene Fathers, it is difficult not to be impressed by their respect and reverence for Scripture as God's inspired, infallible Word. To be sure, there are certain figures, such as Origen, who say a great deal about the irrationality of accepting certain parts of Scripture literally,[15] but who, nevertheless, affirm their belief in the divine origin of God's Word.[16]

Donald W. Dayton, in his review of *The Battle for the Bible*, objects to what he calls Lindsell's "linchpin argument that the church has always held to the inerrancy of Scripture just as Lindsell understands it." He charges that Lindsell has presented a "one dimensional analysis which is supported by a carefully arranged pastiche of quotations wrenched from their context." Dayton maintains that Lindsell "fails to indicate the contrary evidence and almost totally ignores the scholarly debate over the interpretation of the material he quotes."[17]

It is significant to note, however, that George Duncan Barry, one who is no friend to the concept of Biblical inerrancy, and who is the source for a great many of Lindsell's quotations and comments, holds that inerrancy was the predominant view during the first five centuries of the church. He writes:

> It was, to our modern judgment, a mechanical and erroneous view of inspiration that was accepted and taught by the

church of the first centuries, seeing that it ruled out all possibility of error in matters either of history or of doctrine. Men expressed their belief in the inspiration and authority of the Bible in language which startles us by its strange want of reserve. The Scriptures were regarded as writings of the Holy Spirit, no room at all being left for the play of the human agent in the Divine hands. The writers were used by Him as a workman uses His tools; in a word, the books, the actual words, rather than the writers were inspired.[18]

Taking into consideration that the above statement is from the pen of one who is openly nonsupportive of inerrancy, it is indeed surprising to note how closely it parallels the opinion of Warfield and others who are charged with misinterpreting the views of the Fathers. Warfield comments:

> . . . this attitude of entire trust in every word of the Scriptures has been characteristic of the people of God from the very foundation of the church. Christendom has always reposed upon the belief that the utterances of this book are properly oracles of God.[19]

Despite the objections of Dayton, Hubbard, La Sor and others, there are numerous figures among the Church Fathers who affirm in their own words concepts of Biblical infallibility which extend to the very words of Scripture. And, it is interesting to note that many of these figures make such affirmations despite the fact that elsewhere they may struggle with seeming contradictions or various questions of interpretation. In many cases, a presuppositional acceptance of scriptural accuracy shines through regardless of interpretive problems. Following are statements from selected Church Fathers which bear upon both the nature of Scripture and the mode of inspiration.

Origen

If any Church Father had difficulty with a "literal" interpretation of Scripture, it was Origen. He is widely acknowledged as one of the most notorious "spiritualizers" in church history, yet in his book, *Against Celsus*, he challenges:

> . . . let him prove that these words [Scripture] were not spoken by the divine Spirit, who filled the souls of the holy prophets. And let him who likes show that those words [opinions of philosophers] which are acknowledged among all men to be human, are superior to those which are proved to be divine and uttered by inspiration.[20]

In his discussion of Matthew 16:12, Origen further asserts that the Holy Spirit was co-worker with the evangelists in the composition of the Gospel, and that, therefore, lapse of memory, error or falsehood was impossible to them.[21] For Origen, his allegorical tendency notwithstanding, the Scriptures were "fully inspired by the Holy Spirit, and there is no passage either in the Law or the Gospel, or the writings of an apostle, which does not proceed from the inspired source of Divine truth."[22]

Irenaeus

The presupposition that Scripture is infallible no matter what the interpretive problems is nowhere seen more clearly than in Irenaeus' *Against Heresies*. In discussing how to best handle difficult problems in Scripture, he advises:

> If, however, we cannot discover explanations of all those things in Scripture which are made the subject of investigation, let us not on that account seek after any other God besides Him who really exists. For this is the very greatest impiety. We should leave things of that nature to God who created us, being most properly assured that the Scriptures are indeed perfect, since they were spoken by the word of God and His Spirit; but we, inasmuch as we are inferior to, and later in existence than, the word of God and His Spirit, are on that very account destitute of the knowledge of His mysteries.[23]

Through his writings, Irenaeus also evidences his belief that "inspiration does not at all do away with individuality or the literary style of the writers of the Bible."[24]

In regard to the extent of inspiration, Irenaeus writes: "Jesus Christ . . . and the apostles . . . are above all falsehood; for a lie has no fellowship with the truth, just as darkness has none with light, but the presence of one shuts out the other."[25] With Irenaeus, then, inspiration guaranteed truthfulness, and "degrees" of inspiration were considered an impossibility. For Irenaeus, the Scriptures stood or fell together:

> We allege . . . against those who do not recognize Paul as an apostle that they should either reject the words of the Gospel which we have come to know through Luke alone, and not make use of them; or else, if they do receive all these they must necessarily admit also that testimony concerning Paul when he [Luke] tells us the Lord spoke at first to him from heaven: "Saul, Saul, why persecutest thou me? . . ." Those who do not accept him [as a teacher], who was chosen by God for this purpose . . . do separate themselves from the company of the apostles.[26]

Justin Martyr

Near the middle of the second century, Justin Martyr in his *Dialogue with Trypho* precludes any possibility of Biblical contradiction, for in answer to Trypho's question concerning Isaiah 42:8 and its interpretation in regard to how God can give glory to another, he writes:

> And I answered, "if you spoke these words, Trypho, and then kept silence in simplicity and with no ill intent, neither repeating what goes before nor adding what comes after, you must be forgiven; but if you have done so because you imagined that you could throw doubt on the passage, in order that I might say the Scriptures contradicted each other, you have erred. But I shall not venture to suppose or to say such a thing; and if a Scripture which appears to be of such a kind be brought forward, and if there be a pretext [for saying] that it is contrary [to some other], since I am entirely convinced that no Scripture contradicts another. I shall admit rather that I do not understand what is recorded, and shall strive to persuade those who imagine that the Scriptures are contrary, to be rather of the same opinion as myself."[27]

Polycarp and Clement

Polycarp, the faithful student of John who chose to die rather than betray Christ, called Scripture "the oracles of the Lord," and called whoever would pervert them "the first-born of Satan."[28]

Clement, in his first epistle to the Corinthians, says concerning Scripture: "Look carefully into the Scriptures, which are the true utterances of the Holy Spirit. Observe that nothing of an unjust or counterfeit character is written in them."[29]

It is significant to note that both Polycarp and Clement were contemporary with the apostles.

Josephus

Although Josephus cannot truly be considered a Church Father, his historical writings have proved to be remarkably reliable, especially as they relate to Jewish history. Commenting on the Old Testament Scriptures, Josephus observes:

> . . . there is no discrepency in what is written, seeing that, on the contrary, the prophets alone had the privilege of obtaining their knowledge of the most remote and ancient history through the inspiration which they owed to God, and committing to writing a clear account of the events of their own time, just as they occurred.[30]

Chrysostom

The fourth century testimony of Chrysostom to the nature of Scripture is that although there is divergence in the historical narrative of the Gospels, "there is no contradiction." He also evidences an awareness that God used human authors to transmit His message to man in the framework of their backgrounds and individual personalities, for he states "that while the writers of the books are inspired, their message is given in their own words, and their individuality is always preserved."[31]

Augustine

Some of the stronger statements made by any Church Father concerning the trustworthiness of Scripture have been preserved for us in the writings of St. Augustine. In chapter I, a clear statement of Augustine's belief has already been cited. That statement, however, is only one of many.

In speaking of the Manicheans, who maintained that many parts of the divine Scriptures are false, Augustine warns of the dangers involved in admitting that the apostles wrote falsehoods. He advises:

> Does your holy prudence not understand what an avenue we open to their malace if we say, not that the Apostolic writings were falsified by others, but that the Apostles themselves wrote falsehoods.[32]

Augustine's strong convictions along this line are also revealed in an objection to St. Jerome's claim in his commentary on Galatians that Paul had used a white lie. He cautions:

> It seems to me that the most disastrous consequences must follow upon our believing that anything false is found in the sacred books: that is to say that the men by whom the Scripture has been given to us and committed to writing, did put down in these anything false. If you once admit into such a high sanctuary of authority one false statement, there will not be left a single sentence of those books, which, if appearing to anyone difficult in practice or hard to believe, may not by the same fatal rule be explained away as a statement, in which, intentionally, the author declared what was not true.[33]

In his analysis of Augustine's position on Scripture, Jack Rogers appears to focus his reader's attention away from Augustine's statements on verbal inspiration. Although he admits, "Scripture was a divine unity for Augustine. No discordancy of any kind was permitted to exist," he goes on to say:

> Varient readings were not an ultimate problem for Augustine because the truth of Scripture resided ultimately in the thought of the Biblical writers and not in their individual words. Augustine commented, "In any man's words the thing which we ought to narrowly regard is only the writer's thought which was meant to be expressed and to which the words ought to be subservient." To keep to the thoughts and intentions of the Biblical writers we must, according to Augustine, remember that their purpose was to bring us, not information in general, but the good news of Salvation.[34]

The real purpose of this quotation by Augustine, however, was to reject the idea that the gospel writers made any incorrect statements, for the conclusion of the quote which Rogers fails to cite makes this clear:

> . . . and further that we should not suppose one to be giving an incorrect statement, if he happens to convey in different

words what the person really meant whose words he fails to reproduce literally.[35]

In the context of these quotations, then, Augustine was attempting to demonstrate the harmony between statements in the Gospels which differ when describing the same event. Further, according to Polman, Rogers' source of information on Augustine's views: "He [Augustine] did not argue from the common experience that a number of people may tell the same story but not with precisely the same words, but rather used the differences between the Gospels to prove that different versions of common events must never be called lies."[36]

Then, in what appears to be a further attempt to use the words of Augustine to support his position against Biblical inerrancy in relation to matters of science, Rogers writes:

> For Augustine, Scripture was not a textbook of science or an academic tract, but the Book of Life, written in the language of Life. When Felix the Manichean claimed that the Holy Spirit had revealed Manicheus the orbits of the heavenly bodies, Augustine replied that God desired us to become Christians, not astronomers. Such talk, Augustine said, "takes up much of our valuable time and thus distracts our attention from more wholesome matters." Although our authors knew the truth about the shape of the heavens, the Spirit of God who spoke by them did not intend to teach men these things, in no way profitable for salvation.[37]

Thus, Rogers leaves the reader with the impression that according to Augustine one is not to place much confidence in scriptural statements which relate to scientific matters. However, contextual examination indicates that Augustine's above statement was intended to correct the Manicheans' tendency to speak concerning matters which are not detailed in Scripture such as, "the shape of the heavens, . . . the orbits of the Moon, the Sun and the stars, . . . whether the Moon and stars are equally bright."[38] Augustine's concern was that many Christians were speaking in ignorance about scientific matters and attempting to support their pronouncements with Biblical data, thus exposing themselves to ridicule. He was also concerned that Christians were leaving the impression that the

Foundations of Biblical Inerrancy / 21

Biblical writers were responsible for their "mutterings, thus discrediting Christianity before the eyes of the world, which is led to assume that the authors of Scripture were ignorant fools also."[39] According to Polman, it seems the Manicheans were using Scripture irresponsibly, for he writes:

> St. Augustine remembered vividly how many telling blows he himself had delivered during his Manichean days against those Christians who lacking thorough instruction yet tried to defend their faith with all their might. Hence he warned the pious not to try to cover up their ignorance of matters of fact by discussing scientific questions with an easy appeal to the Scriptures.[40]

In relation to Augustine's true opinion on science and Scripture, Polman writes:

> St. Augustine was fully convinced that there can be no discrepancy between the revelations of Scripture and the manifest evidence of reason: "For if reason be found contradicting the authority of the Divine Scriptures, it only deceives by a semblance of truth, however acute it be, for its deductions cannot in that case be true. On the other hand, if, against the most manifest and reliable testimony of reason, anything be set up claiming to have the authority of the Holy Scriptures, he who does this does it through a misapprehension of what he has read, and is setting up against the truth not the real meaning of Scripture, which he has failed to discover, but an opinion of his own; he alleges not what he has found in the Scriptures but what he has found in himself as their interpreter" [Letters, 143, 7]. Whenever, therefore, the nature of things is discovered by reliable investigation, these discoveries will always be capable of being reconciled with the Scripture. Quotations from profane authors that are apparently opposed to the Scriptures must, according to our Catholic faith, be utterly refuted.[41]

Because Polman's interpretation of Augustine's views on the nature of Scripture is so different from the way in which Rogers represents it, this writer feels it imperative to include the heavily documented quotation from Polman which follows:

> St. Augustine was fully convinced that the Scriptures were entirely God's work [De civitate Dei XXI, 6, 7]. Everything in the Old and New Testaments was written by one Spirit [Contra Adimantum 3,3] and must hence be believed beyond all doubt

[De civitate Dei XI, 7]. Any suggestion of partial inspiration was rejected out of hand. Divine inspiration provided not only the religious and moral tone of the Scriptures, but it contained quite literally everything that God has revealed to man. In the Scriptures, even historical events are related by divine authority, and must therefore be believed absolutely. What the Scriptures tell of history must be believed firmly and whatever disagrees with the Scriptural accounts must be rejected as utterly false [De civitate Dei XVIII, 40]. This is also true of the account of Creation. "That God made the world we can believe from no one more safely than from God Himself. But where have we heard Him? Nowhere more distinctly than in the Holy Scriptures, where His prophet said: In the beginning God created the heavens and the earth. Was the prophet present? No, but the wisdom of God, by whom all things were made, was there and wisdom insinuates itself into holy souls and makes them the friends of God and his Prophets and noiselessly informs them of his works" [De civitate XI, 4; see also Confessions XII, 24 ff]. True, the Bible does not describe the Creation in detail, but merely tells us what the Holy Ghost in the Biblical author saw needful to report [De Genesi ad litteram V, 23]. What the Scriptures say on the subject is completely reliable, and even when they tell us that a single source watered the whole earth we have no reason for disbelief. Our interpretation may be false, and we must do our utmost to look for an explanation which is in agreement with the Scriptures, for they are undoubtedly truthful even when their truth cannot be demonstrated [De Genesi ad litteram V, 24]. When the Bible tells us that there were waters above the firmament, waters there must have been. In any case, the authority of the Scriptures surpasses the capacity of all our reason [De Genesi ad litteram, II, 9].

This is equally true of the purely historical accounts. Whatever the Scriptures tell of Enoch, Elijah and Moses is absolutely true [Contra Faustum XXVI, 3]. Admittedly, St. Augustine believed—and Dorsch has discussed this point in detail—that the Scriptures contained different literary forms, which all interpreters must take into account. Thus he distinguished between prophetic and profane, and again between prophetic and historical accounts, while holding that these differences in no way detracted from the Bible's reliability. "All that is given as history, is written with historical diligence [De civitate Dei XVII, 1] and with prophetic authority [De civitate Dei XI, 8]. Therefore the chronology of the Holy Scripture is absolutely trustworthy" [De civitate Dei XII, 10]. At first, St. Augustine generally subordinated the historical meaning to a spiritual meaning which he would derive by way of strange allegorical interpretations, but he later accepted the full historical truth of Biblical events [Costello, Diss. *St. Augustine's Doctrine on the Inspiration and Canonicity of Scripture*, Washington, 1930] and defended them staunchly, particularly against the attacks of Faustus, the Manichean. Wherever the Bible states facts clearly, these facts are indisputable and put an end to all arguments. Hence he told Faustus, who denied the Biblical account of Christ's birth: "The reason of our believing Christ to have been born of the Virgin Mary, is not that he could not otherwise have appeared among men in a true body, but because it is so written in the Scripture, which we must believe in order to be saved . . ." [Contra Faustum XXVI, 7].[42]

This writer has found no more persuasive testimony to the fact of St. Augustine's belief in Biblical inerrancy than the above evidence presented by Polman. It appears that Rogers has either knowingly or unknowingly slanted the views of Augustine. At best, he has failed to represent them adequately.

The Consensus of the Reformers

Having examined various statements of the Church Fathers relative to the nature of Scripture, our task now is to determine whether Biblical inerrancy was an integral part of Reformation theology or a post-Reformation development, as charged by Rogers and other opponents of inerrancy.[43] There are, of course, volumes of opinions concerning the Reformers' views on the nature of Scripture. The safest technique to employ in ascertaining the Reformers' actual views, however, is to examine the words of the Reformers themselves.

Luther

Although Luther and other Reformers never felt compelled to credalize their belief in Biblical inerrancy, there is, nevertheless, an abundance of evidence indicating that such was the position of Luther. Bodamer, in his article, "Luthers Sellung Zur Lehre Von der Verbalinspiration" says:

Read only volumes I-IX and XIV and you will find more than a thousand statements of Luther which unequivocally assert verbal inspiration and identify Scripture and the Word of God.[44]

In his essay, "The Babylonian Captivity of the Church," Luther reveals his high regard for the words of Scripture. He writes:

> No violence is to be done to the words of God, whether by man or angel; but they are to be retained in their simplest meaning wherever possible, and to be understood in their grammatical and literal sense unless the context plainly forbids; lest we give our adversaries occasion to make a mockery of all the Scriptures. Thus Origen was repudiated in olden times, because he despised the grammatical sense and turned the trees, and all things else concerning Paradise, into allegories,; for it might therefrom be concluded that God did not create trees.[45]

Speaking of his shift in interpretive methodology as his scholarship matured, Luther avers:

> . . . When I was young I was learned, especially before I came to the study of theology. At that time I dealt with allegories, Tropologies, and analogies and did nothing but clever tricks with them. If somebody had them today they'd be looked upon as rare relics. I know they're nothing but rubbish. Now I've let them go and this is my last and best art, to translate the Scriptures in their plain sense. The literal sense does it—in it there's life, comfort, power, instruction, and skill. The other is tomfoolery, however brilliant the impression it makes.[46]

Concerning the exclusive trustworthiness of Scripture, Luther quotes St. Augustine in his essay, "On Councils and the Churches." He observes:

> St. Augustine . . . says, in the letter to St. Jerome, which Gratian also quotes, . . . "I have learned to hold the Scriptures alone inerrant; all others, I so read that however holy or learned they may be, I do not hold what they teach to be true, unless they prove, from Scripture or reason, that it must be so." Furthermore, in the same section of the *Decretum* is St. Augustine's saying, from the preface to his book *De trinitate*, "Do not follow my writings as holy Scripture. When you find in Holy Scripture anything that you did not believe before, believe it without doubt; but in my writings, you should hold nothing for certain, concerning which you were before uncertain, unless I

have proved that it is certain." Many more sayings of this kind are in other passages of his writings.[47]

Following his quotation of the above statement, Luther endorses it by declaring, "The Scriptures have never erred" (XV:1481). Elsewhere in his works, Luther writes:

> It is impossible that Scripture should contradict itself. It appears to do so only to senseless and obstinate hypocrites.[48]
>
> Everyone knows that at times they [the fathers] have erred as men will; therefore, I am ready to trust them only when they prove their opinions from Scripture, which has never erred.[49]
>
> Mr. Wiseacre is a shameful, disgusting fellow. He plays the master if he can discover that [in our Bible translation] we have perchance missed a word. But who would be so presumptuous as to maintain that he has not erred in any word, as though he were Christ and the Holy Spirit?[50]

Engelder, in his classic work, *The Scripture Cannot be Broken*, quotes Luther as follows:

> One little point of doctrine means more than heaven and earth, and therefore we cannot suffer to have the least jot thereof violated (IX:650) . . . . For it is established by God's Word that God does not lie, nor does His word lie (XX:798).[51]

Engelder continues by observing, "Luther was so filled with awe of the sacredness of Scripture that he would not and could not admit the possibility of errors and contradictions in Scripture . . . ."[52]

In relation to whether the Bible might still be considered trustworthy when parts of it may not be true, Luther writes:

> No man will take stock in a book or writing parts of which are untrue, particularly if he cannot tell which parts are true and which are untrue (XX:2275).[53]

In spite of the statements quoted above, there are still those who insist on claiming Luther in support of their crusade against Biblical inerrancy. Some argue that Luther's strong affirmations of scriptural authority apply only to its *Christic* content, which he experienced so deeply. And as for the Biblical "details," Luther was impatient with them, and should, therefore, not be regarded as a modern plenary inspirationist. Concerning this view, Montgomery writes:

This is the position espoused by Kostlin in his standard older treatment of Luther's theology, and more recently by the Dutch Lutheran-scholar Kooiman in his influential book, *Luther and the Bible*. Philip Watson, in his otherwise masterly study, *Let God be God!* writes: "For Luther all authority belongs ultimately to Christ, the Word of God, alone, and even the authority of Scriptures is secondary and derivative, pertaining to them only inasmuch as they bear witness to Christ and are the vehicle of the Word." Neo-orthodox theologian, J. K. S. Reid echoes this theme concluding: "For Luther, Scripture is not the Word, but only witness to the Word, and it is from Him whom it conveys that it derives the authority it enjoys."[54]

Commenting on this interpretation of Luther's bibliology, Montgomery avers, "the view is simply not Luther's." He continues:

> To argue that Luther located the trustworthiness of Scripture only in its theological or Christic aspect, not in its *details*, is to misunderstand the very heart of the Reformer's conception of the Bible. It was his belief, from the days of his earliest theologizing, that "the whole Scripture is about Christ alone everywhere."[55]

Evidencing his exasperation with the many misrepresentations of Luther's position, Engelder writes:

> It is one of the mysteries of the ages how theologians who claim to be conversant with Luther's writings can give credence to the myth that Luther did not teach verbal, plenary inspiration. A hundred years ago [1840] Rudelbach dealt with this phenomenon. The myth which has no basis in Luther's writings—as Rudelbach conclusively shows—will not die (Zeitschrift f.d. qesm. Luth. Theol. u. Kirche, 1840, zweites Quartalh, p. 6) . . . . The moderns are going to believe the myth till doomsday.[56]

The myth will not die and has not died to this day largely because one of the weaknesses of human theologians is the obsession to have great men agree with them. Along this line, Montgomery observes:

> It is most interesting to observe that a Neo-Orthodox such as Brunner discovers a Luther who refuses to identify "the letters and words of the Scriptures with the Word of God," while a Post-Bultmannian advocate of the New Hermeneutic, such as Ebeling, finds a Luther who devotes himself "to the service of

the word-event in such a way that the word becomes truly word." How easy it is to meet a Luther who is one's own mirror image.[57]

This tendency, according to Montgomery, is especially strong among those whose theological positions allow such transformations in principle, that is, among liberal theologians who will not accept an objective, determinative standard for their beliefs, but allow personal experience a constitutive role in the creation of theology. Concerning such theologians, Montgomery writes, "[They] . . . are used to bending Scripture to fit their own ideas or the dictates of the Zeitgeist, so performing the same operation on Luther comes easy."[58]

It is interesting to note that Adolf von Harnack, the great rationalist historian of dogma, is critical of Luther for being too narrow in his doctrine of inspiration. He charges:

> He [Luther] confounded the word of God and the Sacred Scriptures and consequently did not break the bondage of the letter. Thus it happened that his church arrived at the most stringent doctrine of inspiration.[59]

It would seem, then, that the *sine qua non* for correcting modern misinterpretations concerning Luther's view of Scripture is to let Luther speak for himself, as we have attempted to do. However, it is precisely at this point that the informed opponents of Luther-as-plenary-inspirationist hasten to inform us that Luther's practice belied his profession where scriptural authority is concerned, for (1) Did not the Reformer handle Scripture with the greatest freedom when he translated it? (2) Was he not primarily concerned with central theological teachings, evidencing a noticeable indifference to contradictions and errors? and (3) Is not his wholesale rejection of certain books from the canon of Scripture irrefutable evidence that he could not possibly have taken every word of the Bible as God's Word? A preliminary answer to such questions is provided by Paul Althaus in his *Theology of Martin Luther*. Althaus, who credits Luther with failing to distinguish "between the Word of God in the true sense and a false biblicism,"[60] writes:

> It is not a question of how far Luther may have gone in one-

sided or forced interpretations of the Scripture. Neither would we speak about his criticism of the canon. These matters do not alter the fact that Luther—even when he criticized Scripture—never wanted to be anything else than a obedient hearer and student of the Scripture.[61]

Along this line, Montgomery comments: "Even if the worst could be shown concerning Luther's treatment of the Bible in practice (which is hardly the case . . .), it would be manifestly unfair to use this to negate his repeated asseverations that he believed in an inerrant Scripture."[62] Then Montgomery proceeds to make the following profound observation:

> Where would any of us be, inconsistent sinners that we are, if our practice were allowed to erase our profession? Just as problem passages in Scripture must not be allowed to swallow up the Bible's clear testimonies to its entire reliability, but must be handled in the light of these testimonies, so Luther's treatment of Scripture must always be viewed from the standpoint of the unequivocal words we have heard him express again and again: "The Scriptures have never erred."[63]

The writer concludes his focus on Luther's view of Scripture with two quotations which are "as typical of him as they are disturbing in the present theological milieu":

> Over against all the statements of the fathers and of all men, yes, over against words of angels and devils, I place the Scriptures.
>
> I have learned to ascribe the honor of infallibility only to those books that are accepted as canonical. I am profoundly convinced that none of these writers have erred.[64]

Calvin

As Calvin lay on his deathbed in 1564, he summarized for his fellow pastors what he had sought to do, and what he believed he had done:

> As for my doctrine, I have taught faithfully, and God has given me grace to write, which I have done faithfully as I could; and I have not corrupted one single passage of Scripture nor twisted it so far as I know; and when I studied subtlety, I have put all that under my feet and have always aimed at being simple. I have written nothing out of hatred against any one, but I

have always set before me what I thought was for the Glory of God."[65]

Such was Calvin's respect for the Scriptures. Yet, to describe the Reformer's view of Scripture is no easy task largely because "with the Apostolic Christians of all ages Calvin confesses the divine inspiration of the Sacred Scriptures. He considers it a catholic truth which is completely beyond dispute . . . . He does not discuss the subject but presupposes it."[66] Calvin's major concern had to do with the message and authority of Scripture—how the Bible sets forth Christ and grace; how the Spirit authenticates the Word of God and interprets it; making it both self-evidencing and clear; and how Christ teaches and rules His people through the ministry of the Word. These were the matters which Calvin debated with the Roman Church, for example, which viewed itself as authenticator and interpreter of the Word, thereby usurping the place of the Holy Spirit; and with the Anabaptists, who went to the opposite extreme of equating "private revelation" with the Scriptures as the instrument of God's rule over peoples' lives. Calvin had no cause, however, to defend Biblical inerrancy or even inspiration against either Rome or the Anabaptists, for neither denied that the Bible came from God. Consequently, Calvin never closely defined his position on the nature of Scripture and this has led various opponents of inerrancy to conclude that he attached little importance to maintaining the total truth of Scripture.[67] Three principle reasons have been suggested by Packer for the difficulty in ascertaining Calvin's precise position on the nature of Scripture.

First, what Calvin does say on Scripture tends often to be paradoxical, and has prompted Bauke, for example, to diagnose his thoughts as *complexio oppositorum*, the intertwining of thoughts which appear to be exclusive of each other.[68] Packer analyzes the problem as:

> . . . a question of relating the numerous passages where he speaks of the Holy Spirit "dictating" the Scriptures to the prophets and apostles, his "amanuenses," and the no less frequent places where he treats the text as a human production and as

such, sometimes incorrect on matters of fact. Some scholars emphasize the one side, some the other. Doumergue will distinguish between the form and content of Scripture and say with Gallican [sic] fervour: "it is not the words that are important, it is the *doctrine*, the spiritual doctrine, the substance." But Professor Dowey considers that Calvin "believes the revelation to have been given word for word by the Spirit." Both views are quite correct and can be supported from Calvin's writings.[69]

Second, as with Luther, scholars have been prone to read their own preoccupations into Calvin. Thus, Reformed theologians quote him in support of their views, and those who stand in a non-Calvinist tradition accuse him of holding positions they have rejected. For example, some opponents of Biblical inerrancy find in Calvin a willingness to go along with them in their denial that all the Bible is true;[70] while others who hold to the fallibility of Scripture convict the Reformer of teaching a "mechanical" view of divine dictation.[71] Still others, in the tradition of Schleiermacher, who see religious consciousness as the true source of theological convictions, have interpreted Calvin's doctrine of the Spirit's inner witness as a foreshadowing of this view.[72]

Third, Calvin never faced the problems contemporary, conservative evangelicals face with those who limit Biblical infallibility to matters of faith and practice.[73]

In spite of the many factors which have clouded Calvin's view of Scripture, there are certain indications that he presupposed inerrancy to be axiomatic, even in his comments concerning "slips in the Biblical text."[74] Packer holds that those who charge the Reformer with a willingness to admit error in Scripture do so on the basis of a "superficial misreading of what he actually says," and he catagorizes passages in Calvin's commentaries which have been used to affirm or imply that the Reformer believed particular writers had gone astray in the following manner:

(1) Some are reminders of points where God has accommodated Himself to rough-and-ready forms of human speech, and tell us only that in such cases God is evidently not concerned to speak with a kind of accuracy which goes beyond

what these forms of speech would naturally convey.

(2) Others say only that particular texts show signs of having been altered in the course of transmission. Thus, for instance, Calvin tells us that "by mistake" Jeremiah's name has somehow "crept in" (*obrepserit*, his regular word for unauthentic textual intrusions) in Matthew 27:9. There is a similar comment on "Abraham" and the seventy-five souls in Acts 7:14-16.

(3) Others deal with cases where apostolic writers quote Old Testament texts loosely; Calvin's point in this group of comments is invariable that the apostles quote paraphrastically precisely in order to bring out the true sense and application—a contention strikingly supported by the modern discovery that this was standard practice among the rabbis at that time.

(4) Others deal with a few points of what we might call formal inaccuracy by suggesting that in these cases no assertion was intended, and therefore no error can fairly be said to have been made . . . . An example of this class of statements is Calvin's denial that the evangelists meant at every point to write narratives which were chronologically ordered, leading to the claim that since they did not intend to connect everything chronologically, but on occasion preferred to follow a topical or theological principle of arrangement, therefore they cannot be held to contradict each other when they narrate the same events in a different sequence. Another example . . . is Calvin's suggestion that in Acts 7:14 (the seventy-five souls) and Hebrews 11:21 (Jacob's staff) the writer may have chosen to echo the Septuagint's mistranslation of the Hebrew of Genesis rather than correct it, lest he disconcert his readers or distract them from the point he was making, which was not affected by the mistranslation one way or the other. In these cases, Calvin implies, alluding to the incidents in the familiar words of the Greek Bible would not involve asserting either that the Septuagint translation was correct or that it expressed the true facts at the point where it parted company from the Hebrew. On neither of these issues would the New Testament writer be himself asserting anything, and consequently his formal inaccuracy in echoing the substantial inaccuracy of the Septuagint would not amount to error (false assertion) on his part.[75]

Packer concludes his explanation of Calvin's methodology with the following statement which this writer holds to be quite significant:

Whether this line of explanation be accepted or not, it is

clear that, so far from admitting that biblical authors fell into error, Calvin's concern in his treatment of all these passages is to show that they did no such thing: and this is what matters for us at present.⁷⁶

Although, as has been demonstrated, Calvin gives no formal analysis of his view of inspiration, in his exposition of II Timothy 3:16, he leaves no doubt that he believes the Scriptures to have come directly from God. He writes:

> He [Paul] commends the Scripture, first, on account of its authority, and second, on account of the utility that springs from it. In order to uphold the authority of Scripture, he declares it to be divinely inspired [*divinitus inspiratam*]: for if it be so, it is beyond all controversy that men should receive it with reverence. . . . Whoever then wishes to profit in the Scriptures, let him first of all lay down as a settled point this—that the law and the prophecies are not teaching [*doctrinam*] delivered by the will of men, but dictated [*dictatam*] by the Holy Ghost . . . . Moses and the prophets did not utter at random what we have from their hand, but, since they spoke by divine impulse, they confidently and fearlessly testified, as was actually the case, that it was the mouth of the Lord that spoke [*os Domini Loguutum esse*] . . . . We owe to the Scripture the same reverence which we owe to God, because it has proceeded from Him alone, and has nothing of man mixed with it [*nec quicquam humani habet admixtum*]. The full authority which they [the Scriptures] obtain with the faithful proceeds from no other consideration than that they are persuaded that they proceeded from heaven, as if God had been heard giving utterance to them.⁷⁶

Concerning the charge that Calvin believed in a mechanical dictation view of inspiration, Kantzer writes:

> Some students of Calvin, among them Warfield, have argued that the reformer does not really teach a true dictation theory of inspiration. Rather, so he explains, Calvin means only to imply that the written Scriptures, which the prophets and apostles composed in the full exercise of their human powers of intellect and emotion and will, are just as much the Word of God as though every word had been immediately dictated.
>
> Whether for forcefulness of the reformer's vocabulary can be adequately accounted for by such an interpretation is open to question; but the broad outlines of Calvin's psychology of inspiration are very transparent. According to him the human

authors of Scripture were controlled by God in every detail of what they wrote.[77]

Given the historical evidence to the contrary, it is indeed difficult to imagine how the concept of Biblical inerrancy can be characterized by Rogers, Hubbard, Rees and others as nothing more than a post-Reformation phenomenon. It would appear rather that post-Reformation theologians only verbalized and clarified a doctrine of Scripture in the tradition of the historic Christian Church.

Chapter 3

The Foundation of Scriptural Testimony

In the previous chapter, it has been demonstrated that there is an abundance of evidence to the effect that "inerrancy" was the dominant concept of the early church in relation to the nature of Scripture. However, to reiterate the precaution already stated, ultimately it must not be the opinions of the Church Fathers or the Reformers which determine doctrine. Rather, doctrine must be built upon the teaching of Scripture. Therefore, any theology of Biblical inspiration must be established upon the foundation of scriptural testimony.

David Allan Hubbard, in the final chapter of *Biblical Authority*, appeals for "fresh exegesis" as an ever-recurring need in Biblical studies. With this we can well agree. However, he then proceeds to discuss several Scripture passages claimed by inerrancy advocates in support of Biblical inerrancy, disregarding the implications they hold for this doctrine.

John 10:34–36

Concerning this passage, Hubbard writes:

> John 10:34–36 may be another passage that deserves careful study. The parenthetical clause "and Scripture cannot be broken" has been frequently cited as a key text in an evangelical view of inspiration. And with good reason: it calls attention to the binding quality of Scripture as the teaching of God. Jesus' argument seems to focus on the authority of His citation from Psalm 82:6. The statement "Scripture cannot be broken" is virtually an appeal on His part to what His Jewish opponents also

believed. His aim is not to teach them new insights into the authority of Scripture, but rather to remind them of what they believed about the authority and applicability of the Scripture— an authority that made it lawful for Him to be called the Son of God.

Again, we would agree with Hubbard up to this point. But, he continues by saying:

> Again, we seem to get no help from this passage for our basic question: the definition of inerrancy. What we do gain is evidence that Jesus and the Jews shared a high view of the *divine character* of the Old Testament and of our obligation to heed its words.[78]

It is at this juncture that the present writer must part company with Hubbard, for it appears that he has spoken too quickly.

In the preceding context, Jesus has just spoken of Himself as one with the Father (John 10:30), whereupon the Jews took up stones to stone Him for blasphemy. To check their accusation, Jesus reminds them that even their judges were called "gods" in Psalm 82:6 because of their official functions, and if it was not blasphemy to call them "gods" how then could it be blasphemy to call Him God whom the Father consecrated and sent into the world? The crucial point in this passage which bears upon inerrancy is Jesus' appeal to a poetical piece of Scripture as Law. The quotation was not from the Pentateuch, nor from any portion of Scripture which was held to contain formal legal contents.[79] Thus, Jesus was ascribing binding legal authority to the entirety of Scripture, and the Scripture, He says, cannot be broken. Commenting on this same passage, Arndt observes:

> And what marks this saying of Jesus as particularly impressive is that it pertains to one word, or expression in the Old Testament, not to a doctrine or a general truth. It teaches that not even single terms employed in the Scriptures can be disregarded, be their function even so subordinate.[80]

Regarding the significance of the word "broken" in John 10:35, Whitcomb writes:

> The word for "broken" here is the common one for breaking the law, or the Sabbath (John 5:18, 7:23, Matt. 5:19), and

the meaning of the declaration is that it is impossible for the Scripture to be annulled, its authority to be withstood, or denied. And the context shows that in the Saviour's view the indefectible authority of Scripture attaches to the very form of expression of its most causal clauses. It belongs to Scripture through and through, down to its most minute particulars, that it is of indefectible authority.[81]

It is only logical to assume that if one word or expression in a Psalm is considered by Christ to have such importance and authority, inspiration must of necessity extend to the very words of Scripture; and unless the process of inspiration runs counter to God's nature or attributes, it must be concluded that what is God-breathed is true and without error. Thus, if inerrancy is not directly stated in John 10:34-36, it is most certainly there by implication.

II Timothy 3:16

In his discussion of this great text on inspiration, Hubbard focuses the attention of his readers on the "equipment" which Paul says is needed by Timothy to withstand the pressures of the difficult days ahead. He concludes his remarks by saying:

> It is enough to say here that Paul in II Timothy 3 concludes from the fact of inspiration that the Scripture is profitable and powerful. Should not this tack help us define what we mean by inerrancy if we choose to use the word?[82]

While Hubbard is correct in saying that Scripture is "inspired therefore profitable to equip," in his limited discussion he has avoided any consideration of what is meant by the phrase "all Scripture," and the word "inspired." This is unfortunate, for if there are any implications in II Timothy 3:16 regarding "inerrancy," they are found in the proper understanding of these terms.

In the preceding context Paul warns Timothy that "in the last days difficult times will come" (II Timothy 3:1). He describes how self-centered, recalcitrant and spiritually powerless men will become (II Timothy 3:2-5). He characterizes the endless quest for knowledge and the opposition to the truth which was to develop (II Timothy 3:6-8). And he promises Timothy that he can expect to be persecuted for "all who desire to live Godly in Christ Jesus will suffer persecution" (II Timothy 3:12). Paul then warns his son in the faith that although evil men and imposters will proceed from bad to worse, not only deceiving but being deceived themselves, he (Timothy) is to continue in the things he has learned and become convinced of, being aware of from whom he has received his knowledge (II Timothy 3:14). Timothy is next reminded of his spiritual heritage, that from childhood he has known the "sacred writings" which are able to give him the wisdom that leads to salvation through faith which is in Christ Jesus (II Timothy 3:15).

It is important to note at this point that it is through "the Scriptures" that one receives the wisdom which leads to salvation. The definite focus of attention in both verses 15 and 16 is on "the Scriptures." Then Paul instructs Timothy concerning the importance of Scripture to his spiritual survival. "All Scripture," he says, "is inspired by God . . . ." (II Timothy 3:16).

To understand the implications of this passage for the doctrine of verbal inspiration, there are four problems which must be considered relative to the phrase, "All Scripture is inspired of God . . .": (1) the meaning of πᾶσα, (2) the meaning of γραφή, (3) the proper positioning of the understood verb, and (4) the meaning of θεόπνευστος.

First, the proper translation of πᾶσα must be discussed. According to Arndt and Gingrich, πᾶσα, when used to modify a singular noun without the article, should be translated "every or each."[83] Hendriksen, however, holds that "the word 'Scripture' can be definite even without the article" (I Peter 2:6, II Peter 1:20). "Similarly," he says, "πᾶς Ἰσραήλ means 'all Israel' (Rom. 11:26)."[84] Kent observes that "γραφή is without the article, thus qualitative and emphasizes that all that can lay claim to the quality of divine Scripture is God breathed."[85]

Actually, whether πᾶσα γραφή is translated "every" or "all" is relatively unimportant to the impact of the phrase. Young comments:

If Paul means "every Scripture" he is looking at the various parts of the Bible, that is, he is considering the Scripture distributively. He is then saying that whatever Scripture we consider, it is inspired of God. On the other hand, if he means "all Scripture," it is clear that his reference is to the Scripture in its entirety. In either case he is saying that whatever may be called Scripture is inspired of God.[86]

Second, the meaning of γραφή must be determined. It is obvious that the term must refer primarily to the Old Testament Scriptures. But does the term refer to more than just Old Testament writings? Houghton believes it does, and he cites three reasons for his position: (1) In verse 15, Paul uses the word γράμματα in reference to the "sacred writings." Concerning this variation in form, Hendriksen writes:

> *All Scripture*, in distinction from the "sacred writings" . . . means everything which through the testimony of the Holy Spirit in the church, is recognized by the church as canonical, that is, authoritative. When Paul wrote these words, the direct reference was to a body of Sacred Literature which even then was comprised of more than the Old Testament.[87]

(2) Paul had already described a New Testament passage (Luke 10:7) as γραφή (c.f. I Timothy 5:18). (3) Paul refers to "all Scripture," in contrast to the "sacred writings" of verse 15. Thus, it appears that the γραφή of verse 16 includes more than the "Sacred Writings" (the Old Testament) of verse 15.[88]

Third, the proper position of the "understood" verb must be ascertained. The alternatives are easily seen in the differing translations rendered by the King James Version and the American Standard Version. The King James renders the phrase, "All scripture is given by inspiration of God and is profitable . . . ." while the American Standard has it, "Every Scripture inspired of God is also profitable . . . ." Although both translations are possible, this writer prefers the King James rendering, which is followed by both the Revised Standard Version and the New American Standard Bible, for this reason: to translate the phrase "Every Scripture inspired of God is profitable" may leave the impression that there may be some Scriptures which are not inspired of God and therefore are not profitable. This understanding could well play right into the hands of inerrancy opponents who promote a distinction between "non-revelatory" and "revelatory" Scripture. Expressing his preference for the King James rendering, Kent writes:

> The K.J.V. and the R.S.V. translations are better than the A.S.V., which renders "every Scripture inspired of God is also profitable." The latter is ambiguous, and while its proponents say it assumes inspiration for Scripture, it is certainly capable of being misunderstood. As Simpson observes, to say every God breathed Scripture is profitable presents a "curious specimen of anticlimax." The omission of the "is" finds a parallel in I Timothy 4:4 where no one translates "every good creature of God is also nothing to be thrown away."[89]

Houghton also comments on the advisibility of following the King James rendering:

> This writer favors placing the verb between "Scripture" and "inspired," translating it, "All Scripture is inspired . . ." because this translation allows the conjunction, καί, to fit the sentence naturally. The American Standard Version which gives the alternate reading, translates καί awkwardly: "Every Scripture inspired of God is also (καί) profitable . . ." If Scripture is also profitable, what else is it, since "also" implies that "profitable" is not Scripture's only characteristic? If one answers that "inspired" is its other quality, then he has placed the verb between "Scripture" and "inspired" and is actually agreeing with the way the King James Version (and this writer) translated the verse.[90]

As a consequence of being inspired, then, Scripture is "profitable for teaching, for reproof, for correction, for training in righteousness that the man of God may be adequate, equipped for every good work." Fairbairn avers:

> . . . the καί is to be taken as *kai consecutivum*, presenting what follows as a consequence growing out of what preceeds . . . . Every Scripture is given by inspiration of God, and hence is profitable; because it is that, then, as a matter of course, it is also this.[91]

Fourth, the implications of the word, θεόπνευστος must be examined, for in this most descriptive word resides a wealth of meaning often ignored by opponents of inerrancy. In his discussion of this term, Warfield makes it clear that the translation, "inspired of God," does not convey the true meaning. Rather, he says, the term speaks of "spiration" or "spiring," indicating that Scripture is neither "breathed into by God" nor the product of divine inbreathing into its human authors. In reality, according to Warfield, Scripture is breathed out by God, "God breathed," "the product of the creative breath of God." Then, II Timothy 3:16 indicates that all or every Scripture is a divine product, and no indication is given as to how God operated in producing them.[92]

In the light of the exegesis given above, it would appear that inerrancy is a logical result of God-breathed authorship, for it is difficult to imagine how God could produce something by means of His creative breath which is errant. Again, this would be contrary to His nature.

II Peter 1:20-21

In his discussion of II Peter 1:20-21, Hubbard makes the statement, "we seem to learn nothing from II Peter about the definition of inerrancy which dominates the current debate."[93] While it is true that this passage does not provide a precise definition of inerrancy, it does say a great deal about how God operated in producing the Scriptures.

In the context of the passage, it is clear that there was a major conflict over authority. False teachers were issuing a call for loyalty based on "cleverly devised tales." In contrast, Peter assures his readers that the "prophetic Word" has been made even more sure by the fact that he and others were eyewitnesses of "His majesty" on the Mount of Transfiguration. Confirming this interpretation, Robertson writes:

> The Transfiguration scene confirmed the Messianic prophecies and made clear the deity of Christ as God's beloved Son. Some with less likelihood take Peter to mean that the word of prophecy is a surer confirmation of Christ's deity than the Transfiguration.[94]

Having established the certainty of the "Prophetic Word," Peter goes on to explain its origin. He writes: "But know this

Foundations of Biblical Inerrancy / 41

first of all, that no prophecy of Scripture is a matter of one's own interpretation." Robertson points out that the verb "is" (γίνεται) actually should be translated "comes" or "springs."⁹⁵ Vincent says it should be "arises or originates."⁹⁶ The phrase, "one's own interpretation," means one's own explanation or "the result of human investigation into the nature of things, the product of the writer's own thinking."⁹⁷ It is clear, then, that Scripture did not originate either "on its own," or as a result of human explanation. Then, tying his thoughts together with γάρ, Peter moves from the negative part of his explanation to the positive: "for no prophecy was ever made by an act of human will, but men moved by the Holy Spirit spoke from God." Concerning this verse, Houghton writes:

> Here in clear terminology, Peter declares that men spoke (and wrote, since Peter refers to προφητεία γραφῆς, "Prophecy of Scripture," or "Prophetic Scripture") when they were being borne along by the Holy Spirit. Peter doesn't say that these men were being borne along while they were *thinking*, but while they were *speaking*. This involves words.⁹⁸

In II Peter 1:21 we have an advance in explanation over II Timothy 3:16, for here we are told that God produced the Scriptures through the instrumentality of men who spake from Him. the term used here for "bearing" or "borne" is φερόμενοι meaning "to bear" or "to carry." Concerning this word, Warfield writes:

> The term used here is a very specific one. It is not to be confounded with guiding, or directing, or controlling, or even leading in the full sense of that word. It goes beyond all such terms, in assigning the effect produced specifically to the active agent. What is borne is taken up by the bearer, and conveyed by the bearer's power, not its own, to the bearer's goal, not its own. The men who spoke from God are here declared therefore, to have been taken up by the Holy Spirit and brought by His power to the goal of His choosing. The things which they spoke under this operation of the Spirit were therefore His things, not theirs.⁹⁹

It is significant to note that the same Greek verb is also used in Acts 27:15 to describe the action of a strong wind, "Euraquilo," upon the ship in which Paul was sailing. Luke says, "we gave way to it and let ourselves be driven along." So, just as the wind, Euraquilo, bore the ship along in a direction over which those inside had no control, the Holy Prophets were borne along by the Holy Spirit toward the goal of a Scripture authored by God through them. Again we ask, could such intimate involvement on the part of the Holy Spirit in producing Scripture have allowed for the production of error? It would seem that the very methodology which God employed precludes such a possibility.

CONCLUSION

In this brief work, the author has attempted to speak to the heart of the inerrancy debate. It has been shown that, contrary to the teaching of evangelicals opposed to inerrancy, the concept of Biblical inerrancy was indeed the historic position of the Church. In addition, it has been demonstrated that although we have no formal statement of inerrancy in Scripture, the concept is implied over and over again by the personal involvement of a God of integrity and truth in such a way that men did not speak or write on their own. Rather the superintending power of God, the Holy Spirit, used their backgrounds, their vocabulary, their personalities, and their cultural peculiarities as he wished to produce His Work through them. They were instruments prepared by Him before the foundation of the world to accomplish His sovereign purpose.

May we ever be aware of the fact that we need not apologize for what God says in His Word, and may the pressures of conformity to secular standards of scholarship never bend our will to the presupposition that God would give us an errant Word.

Endnotes

1. Donald Dayton, "Wrong Front: A Review of 'The Battle for the Bible,'" *Theology News and Notes* (Pasadena: Fuller Theological Seminary, Special Issue, 1976), p. 19.
2. Clark Pinnock, Quoted in "News and Views," *Eternity* (November, 1977), p. 90.
3. *Ibid.*
4. John Warwick Montgomery, "Whither Biblical Inerrancy," *Christianity Today* (July 29, 1977), p. 41.
5. David Allen Hubbard, "What We Believe and Teach," *Theology News and Notes*, p. 4.
6. William Sanford La Sor, "Life Under Tension," *Theology News and Notes*, p. 5.
7. Hubbard, *Theology News and Notes*, p. 4.
8. David Allen Hubbard, "The Current Tensions: Is There a Way Out?" *Biblical Authority*, ed. by Jack Rogers (Waco, Texas: Word Books, 1977), p. 165.
9. R. C. Sproul, "The Case for Inerrancy: A Methodological Analysis," *God's Inerrant Word*, ed. by John Warwick Montgomery (Minneapolis: Bethany Fellowship, Inc., 1974), p. 257.
10. Hubbard, *Biblical Authority*, p. 151.
11. Augustine, "Letter 82," trans. by J. G. Cunningham, *Nicene and Post-Nicene Fathers*, ed. by Phillip Schaff (Buffalo: The Christian Literature Company, 1886), I, p. 350.
12. Benjamin B. Warfield, *The Inspiration and Authority of the Bible* (Philadelphia: The Presbyterian and Reformed Publishing Company, 1948), p. 173.
13. Edward J. Young, *Thy Word is Truth* (Grand Rapids: Wm. B. Eerdmans Publishing Company, 1957), p. 139.
14. *Ibid.*
15. Origen, *The Ante-Nicene Fathers*, IV, I, p. 365.
16. *Ibid.*, IV, I, p. 354.
17. Dayton, *Theology News and Notes*, p. 18.
18. George Duncan Barry, *The Inspiration and Authority of Holy Scripture, A Study in the Literature of the First Five Centuries* (New York: Macmillan, 1919), p. 10.
19. Warfield, p. 107.
20. Origen, *The Ante-Nicene Fathers*, *Against Celsus*, III, LXXXI, p. 496.
21. Warfield, p. 108.
22. Barry, pp. 79, 80. (Homilies in Jeremiah, XXI: Philocalia, C, X, II, X).
23. Irenaeus, *The Ante-Nicene Fathers*, I, *Irenaeus Against Heresies*, II, 28, 2, 399.
24. Barry, pp. 54, 56, 57.
25. John F. Walvoord, *Inspiration and Interpretation* (Grand Rapids: Wm. B. Eerdmans Publishing Company, 1957), p. 20.
26. *Ibid.*
27. Justin Martyr, *The Ante-Nicene Fathers*, I, *Dialogue With Trypho*, pp. 65, 230.
28. Polycarp, *The Ante-Nicene Fathers*, I, *The Epistle of Polycarp*, VII, p. 34.
29. Clement, *The Ante-Nicene Fathers*, I, *The First Epistle of Clement*, XLV, 17.

30. Josephus, *Against Apion*, I, Loeb Classical Library; pp. 37-40.
31. Barry, pp. 121-24.
32. Augustinus, Letters I, *The Fathers of the Church*, ed. by Joseph Deferrari, et al, trans. by Sister Wilfred Parsons (Washington, D.C., The Catholic University of America Press, 1951), p. 394.
33. Augustine, *Nicene and Post-Nicene Fathers*, I, *Letters of St. Augustine*, ed. by Phillip Schaff, trans. by J. G. Cunningham, Letter II, 28:3 (Buffalo: The Christian Literature Company, 1886), pp. 251-52.
34. Rogers, *Biblical Authority*, p. 21.
35. A. D. R. Polman, *The Word of God According to St. Augustine*, trans. by A. J. Pomerans (Grand Rapids: Wm. B. Eerdmans Publishing Company, 1961), p. 49.
36. *Ibid.*, p. 48.
37. Rogers, *Biblical Authority*, pp. 21, 22.
38. Polman, pp. 59-60.
39. *Ibid.*, p. 61.
40. *Ibid.* (De duabus animis II).
41. *Ibid.*, pp. 60, 61. (Epistula 143, 7; De Genesi ad litteram I, 41).
42. *Ibid.* pp. 52, 53.
43. Rogers, pp. 29, 30.
44. Theodore Engelder, *Scripture Cannot Be Broken* (St. Louis: Concordia Publishing House, 1944), p. 291.
45. Hugh Thompson Kerr, Jr. *A Compend of Luther's Theology* (Philadelphia: The Westminster Press, 1943), p. 17.
46. Martin Luther, *Luther's Works*, 54, *Table Talk* (Philadelphia: Fortress Press, 1967), p. 406.
47. Kerr, pp. 15, 16.
48. John Warwick Montgomery, "Lessons from Luther on the Inerrancy of Holy Writ," *God's Inerrant Word*, p. 66. (Weimarer Ausgabe, 9, 356).
49. *Ibid.*, p. 67. (Weimarer Ausgabe, 7, 315).
50. *Ibid.* (Weimarer Ausgabe, 38, 16).
51. Engelder, pp. 33, 37.
52. *Ibid.*
53. *Ibid.*, p. 211.
54. Montgomery, *God's Inerrant Word*, p. 66.
55. *Ibid.*, p. 67.
56. Engelder, pp. 290-91.
57. Montgomery, p. 69.
58. *Ibid.*
59. Adolf von Harnack, *Outlines of the History of Dogma,* trans. by Edwin Knox Mitchell (Boston: Beacon Press, 1957), pp. 561-62.
60. Paul Althaus, *The Theology of Martin Luther*, trans. by Robert C. Schultz (Philadelphia: Fortress Press, 1966), pp. 50-52.
61. *Ibid.*, p. 5.
62. Montgomery, p. 70.
63. *Ibid.* For a detailed answer to the three questions posed by opponents of Luther-as-Plenary-Inspirationist, see *God's Inerrant Word*, pp. 70-84.
64. *Ibid.*, p. 90.

65. J. I. Packer, "Calvin's View of Scripture," *God's Inerrant Word*, pp. 95-96.
66. A. D. R. Polman, "Calvin on the Interpretation of Scripture," *John Calvin Contemporary Prophet*, ed. by J. T. Hoogstra (Grand Rapids: Baker Book House, 1959), pp. 97, 102.
67. Packer, *God's Inerrant Word*, p. 98.
68. *Ibid.*, p. 96. (H. Bauke die Probleme der Theologie Calvins, Leipzig: J. C. Hinrichs, 1922).
69. *Ibid.*, pp. 96, 97. (T. H. L. Parker, *Calvin's New Testament Commentaries*, London: S C M, 1971, p. 53).
70. C. A. Briggs, *The Bible, the Church and Reason* (New York: Scribners, n.d.), pp. 24, 219.
71. R. E. Davies, *The Problem of Authority in the Continental Reformers* (London: Epworth, 1946), p. 114.
72. Packer, *God's Inerrant Word*, p. 97.
73. Hubbard, *Biblical Authority*, p. 170.
74. Packer, *God's Inerrant Word*, p. 98.
75. *Ibid.*, p. 106-07.
76. *Ibid.*, p. 107.
77. Kenneth Kantzer, "Calvin and the Holy Scriptures," *Inspiration and Interpretation*, p. 140.
78. Hubbard, *Biblical Authority*, p. 173.
79. John C. Whitcomb, *Contemporary Theology* (Unpublished Class Notes, Grace Theological Seminary, Fall, 1977), p. 53.
80. William F. Arndt, *Bible Difficulties* (St. Louis: Concordia Publishing House, 1932), pp. 4-5.
81. Whitcomb, p. 54.
82. Hubbard, *Biblical Authority*, p. 174.
83. William F. Arndt and F. Wilbur Gingrinch, *A Greek-English Lexicon of the New Testament and other Early Christian Literature* (Chicago: University of Chicago Press, 1957), p. 636.
84. William Hendriksen, *New Testament Commentary: Exposition of the Pastoral Epistles* (Grand Rapids: Baker Book House, 1965), p. 301.
85. Homer A. Kent Jr., *The Pastoral Epistles* (Chicago: Moody Press, 1958), p. 290.
86. Edward J. Young, *Thy Word is Truth* (Grand Rapids: Wm. B. Eerdmans Publishing Company, 1957), p. 19.
87. Hendriksen, p. 301.
88. Myron James Houghton, *New Testament Teaching on the Inspiration and Inerrancy of Scripture* (Unpublished Master of Theology Thesis, Grace Theological Seminary, 1968), pp. 63, 64.
89. Kent, p. 290.
90. Houghton, p. 64.
91. Patrick Fairbairn, *Commentary on the Pastoral Epistles* (Grand Rapids: Zondervan Publishing House, 1956), p. 380.
92. Warfield, p. 133.
93. Hubbard, *Biblical Authority*, p. 175.
94. A. T. Robertson, *Word Pictures in the New Testament*, VI (Nashville: Broadman Press, 1933), pp. 157-58.

95. *Ibid.*, p. 158.
96. Marvin R. Vincent, *Word Studies in the New Testament* (Grand Rapids: Wm. B. Eerdmans Publishing Company, 1946), I, p. 688.
97. Whitcomb, p. 52.
98. Houghton, p. 78.
99. Warfield, p. 137.

Bibliography

Althaus, Paul. *The Theology of Martin Luther.* Trans. by Robert C. Schultz. Philadelphia: Fortress Press, 1966.
Arndt, William F. *Bible Difficulties.* St. Louis: Concordia Publishing House, 1932.
Arndt, William F. and Gingrinch, F. Wilbur. *A Greek-English Lexicon of the New Testament and Other Early Christian Literature.* Chicago: University of Chicago Press, 1957.
Augustine. *Nicene and Post-Nicene Fathers.* Ed. by Phillip Schaff. Trans. by J. G. Cunningham. Buffalo: The Christian Literature Company, 1886.
Augustinus. *Fathers of the Church.* Ed. by Joseph Deferrari, et al. Trans. by Sister Wilfred Parsons. Washington, D.C.: The Catholic University of America Press, 1951.
Barry, George Duncan. *The Inspiration and Authority of Holy Scripture, A Study in the Literature of the First Five Centuries.* New York: Macmillan, 1919.
Briggs, C. A. *The Bible, the Church and Reason.* New York: Scribners, n.d.
Clement. *The Ante-Nicene Fathers.* Vol. I. *The First Epistle of Clement.* New York: Scribners, 1899.
Davies, R. E. *The Problem of Authority in the Continental Reformers.* London: Epworth, 1946.
Dayton, Donald. "Wrong Front: A Review of 'The Battle for the Bible.' " *Theology News and Notes.* Pasadena: Fuller Theological Seminary, Special Issue, 1976.
Engelder, Theodore. *Scripture Cannot Be Broken.* St. Louis: Concordia Publishing House, 1944.
Fairbairn, Patrick. *Commentary on the Pastoral Epistles.* Grand Rapids: Zondervan Publishing House, 1956.
Geisler, Norman L. and Nix, William E. *A General Introduction to the Bible.* Chicago: Moody Press, 1968.
Harnack, Adolf von. *Outlines of the History of Dogma.* Trans. by Edwin Knox Mitchell. Boston: Beacon Press, 1966.
Hendriksen, William. New Testament Commentary: *Exposition of the Pastoral Epistles.* Grand Rapids: Baker Book House, 1965.
Houghton, Myron James. *New Testament Teaching on the Inspiration and Inerrancy of Scripture.* Unpublished Master of Theology Thesis, Grace Theological Seminary, 1968.
Hubbard, David Allen. "The Current Tensions: Is There a Way Out?" *Biblical Authority.* Ed. by Jack Rogers. Waco, Texas: Word Books, 1977.
Hubbard, David Allen. "What We Believe and Teach." *Theology News and Notes.* Pasadena: Fuller Theological Seminary, Special Issue, 1976.
Irenaeus. *The Ante-Nicene Fathers.* Vol. I. *Irenaeus Against Heresies.* Ed. by Alexander Roberts and James Donaldson. Grand Rapids: Wm. B. Eerdmans Publishing Company, 1950.
Josephus. *Against Apion.* Trans. by H. St. J. Thackeray. Vol. I of *Loeb Classical Library.* Cambridge: Harvard University Press, 1956.
Kantzer, Kenneth. "Calvin and the Holy Scriptures." *Inspiration and Interpretation.* Grand Rapids: Wm. B. Eerdmans Publishing Company, 1957.

Kent, Homer A. Jr. *The Pastoral Epistles*. Chicago: Moody Press, 1958.
Kerr, Hugh Thomson, Jr. *A Compend of Luther's Theology*. Philadelphia: The Westminster Press, 1943.
La Sor, William Sanford. "Life Under Tension." *Theology News and Notes*. Pasadena: Fuller Theological Seminary, Special Issue, 1976.
Lindsell, Harold. *The Battle For The Bible*. Grand Rapids: Zondervan Publishing House, 1976.
Luther, Martin, *Luther's Works. Vol. 54. Table Talk*. Ed. and Trans. by Theodore G. Tappert. Philadelphia: Fortress Press, 1967.
Montgomery, John Warwick. "Lessons from Luther on the Inerrancy of Holy Writ." *God's Inerrant Word*. Ed. by the author. Minneapolis: Bethany Fellowship, Inc., 1974.
Montgomery, John Warwick. "Whither Biblical Inerrancy." *Christianity Today*, July 29, 1977, p. 41.
Martyr, Justin. *The Ante-Nicene Fathers*. Vol. I. *Dialogue With Trypho*. Ed. by Alexander Roberts and James Donaldson. Grand Rapids: Wm. B. Eerdmans Publishing Company, 1950.
Origen, *The Ante-Nicene Fathers*. Vol. III. *Against Celsus*. Ed. by Alexander Roberts and James Donaldson. Grand Rapids: Wm. B. Eerdmans Publishing Company, 1951.
Origen, *The Ante-Nicene Fathers*. Vol. IV. Ed. by Alexander Roberts and James Donaldson. Grand Rapids: Wm. B. Eerdmans Publishing Company, 1951.
Packer, J. I. "Calvin's View of Scripture." *God's Inerrant Word*. Ed. by John Warwick Montgomery. Minneapolis: Bethany Fellowship, Inc., 1974.
Pinnock, "News and Views." *Eternity*. November 7, 1977, p. 90.
Polycarp. *The Ante-Nicene Fathers*. Vol. I. The Epistle of Polycarp. Ed. by Alexander Roberts and James Donaldson. Grand Rapids: Wm. B. Eerdmans Publishing Company, 1950.
Polman, A. D. R. "Calvin on the Interpretation of Scripture." *John Calvin Contemporary Prophet*. Ed. by J. T. Hoogstra. Grand Rapids: Baker Book House, 1959.
Polman, A. D. R. *The Word of God According to St. Augustine*. Trans. by A. J. Pomerans. Grand Rapids: Wm. B. Eerdmans Publishing Company, 1961.
Robertson, A. T. *Word Pictures in the New Testament*. 6 Vols. Nashville: Broadman Press, 1933.
Rogers, Jack, ed. *Biblical Authority*. Waco, Texas: Word Books, 1977.
Sproul, R. C. "The Case for Inerrancy: A Methodological Analysis." *God's Inerrant Word*. Ed. by John Warwick Montgomery. Minneapolis: Bethany Fellowship, Inc., 1974.
Vincent, Marvin R. *Word Studies in the New Testament*. Grand Rapids: Wm. B. Eerdmans Publishing Company, 1946.
Walvoord, John F. *Inspiration and Interpretation*. Grand Rapids: Wm. B. Eerdmans Publishing Company, 1957.
Warfield, Benjamin B. *The Inspiration and Authority of the Bible*. Philadelphia: The Presbyterian and Reformed Publishing Company, 1948.
Whitcomb, John C. *Contemporary Theology*. Unpublished Class Notes. Winona Lake: Grace Theological Seminary, Fall, 1977.
Young, Edward J. *Thy Word is Truth*. Grand Rapids: Wm. B. Eerdmans Publishing Company, 1957.

The BMH Discussion Series

DOES GOD WANT CHRISTIANS TO PERFORM MIRACLES TODAY? By Dr. John C. Whitcomb, professor of theology and Old Testament at Grace Theological Seminary. An analysis of today's faith healers and miracle workers.

DID CHRIST DIE ONLY FOR THE ELECT? By Dr. Charles R. Smith, associate professor of Greek and theology at Grace Theological Seminary. A scholarly and logical treatment of questions regarding the limited atonement and human responsibilities.

CHRIST, OUR PATTERN AND PLAN. By Dr. John C. Whitcomb. An analysis of evangelical missions and evangelism in the light of the Great Commission.

IS THE UNITED STATES IN PROPHECY? By Dr. Herman A. Hoyt, president emeritus of Grace Schools. This booklet reveals answers to questions many people have been asking.

DEMONS, EXORCISM AND THE EVANGELICAL. By Dr. John J. Davis, executive vice president of Grace Schools. An enlightening discussion of demons as personal beings, the practice of exorcism, and an answer to the question: "Can believers be possessed?"

CAN YOU KNOW GOD'S WILL FOR YOUR LIFE? By Dr. Charles R. Smith. A fresh and informative guide to help the reader determine and have assurance regarding the will of God for his or her life.

A CAPSULE VIEW OF THE BIBLE. By W. Russell Ogden, pastor of the First Brethren Church, Lanham, Maryland. A unique booklet enabling the reader to grasp an overview of the contents of the Bible. Ideal for the individual who desires to see the Bible as a whole unit.

— — — — — — — — — — — — — ORDER FORM — — — — — — — — — — — — —

All booklets in this BMH Discussion Series are 16 pages, paperback, and priced at 50c each. SPECIAL OFFER—all seven for $3.25, postage paid, when you include a check with your order.

☐ Please send all seven for $3.25.

☐ Please send _____

_____

(Minimum order, $3.00. Please include your check with order and we pay postage charges.)

Send to: Brethren Missionary Herald Co., P. O. Box 544, Winona Lake, Indiana 46590.